THE PARTS OF A MANOR HOUSE

WRITTEN AND ILLUSTRATED
BY
SIDNEY H. HEATH
ART MASTER, PLYMOUTH COLLEGE
AUTHOR OF "PILGRIM LIFE IN THE MIDDLE AGES,"
"OUR HOMELAND CHURCHES," ETC., ETC.

LONDON

1928

CONTENTS

CHAPTER		PAGE
I.	About Manor Houses	3
II.	The Hall	13
III.	The Kitchen and Offices	19
IV.	Gatehouses and Chapels	23
V.	Doorways and Windows	29
VI.	Chimneys and Fireplaces	35
VII.	Stairways	40
VIII.	Dovecots and Sundials	44

THE PARTS OF A MANOR HOUSE

CHAPTER I

About Manor Houses

IN this little book the term *manor* house is used as meaning the dwelling-place of the lord of the manor, the manor being usually land or estates granted originally by the King to one of his subjects in return for certain services rendered. For example, Elena de Gorges held the manor of Bradpole, in Dorset, by the service of finding an armed esquire, when war should happen, for forty days; and Ralph de Stopham held the manor of Bryanston by the service of finding for our lord the King, as often as he should lead his army into Wales, a boy carrying a bow without a string and an arrow without feathers, at his own cost, for forty days.

Similarly, William the Moigne held the manor of Owres of our lord the King by the service of being caterer in the King's kitchen and keeper of his larder.

Many of these old customs have survived in the services still rendered by certain noblemen at the coronation of a King or Queen.

The usual custom of the manor was for the lord to hold half the land, the other half being divided between the franklins, or freeholders, and the villeins, or serfs.

It was not until the coming of the Normans that small manor houses began to be built in various parts of the country, but there were never a great number of

4 THE PARTS OF A MANOR HOUSE

them, as the nobles for the most part lived in strong castles.

The lord of a manor ruled his estates much as the King ruled the country. He held his own courts, in which he could fine, flog, imprison, and even put to death such of his serfs as offended against the law and customs.

When houses were first built in remote country districts they were generally strongly fortified, but this was not always the case, as there are a few very old manor houses that can show nothing in the way of defence beyond strong walls and doorways. It was on the Welsh and Scottish borderlands, at the junction of high-roads, and at the fording-places of rivers that the greater number of fortified manor houses were built.

Many of these old houses are called castles (for example, Woodsford Castle, Stokesay Castle); but they are nothing more than fortified manor houses which came to be called castles from the tops of the walls having been *castellated*, that is, fitted with battlements.

To embattle a wall or a tower it was necessary to obtain a licence from the King, and to do so without permission was regarded as an act of rebellion. On the Borderlands permission to embattle walls was given by the Lords Marchers in the name of the King. We can quite understand that the King should object to his nobles turning their houses into little fortresses without his knowledge.

In the reign of Edward II, William Montacute, Earl of Sarum (Salisbury), was granted a licence to embattle his house at Kersyngton, in Oxfordshire, and in the following reign he was granted a pardon by

ABOUT MANOR HOUSES

Front

Back

A Moated Manor House

6 THE PARTS OF A MANOR HOUSE

Edward III for embattling a part of his house at Doneygate, in Somerset, without licence.

The first of the outer defences was the moat, filled with water from a neighbouring stream. This moat surrounded the house on every side, the only way across it being by means of a bridge of wood and, in later days, of stone. There was often a *drawbridge*, but this did not extend the full width of the moat. It merely filled the gap left between the end of the stone bridge nearest the house, and the doorway.

The entrance doorway was usually placed in a strong tower and protected with a portcullis, or iron grating, which, like the drawbridge, could be raised or lowered at will.

On the roof of the entrance tower, and sometimes all round the tops of the outside walls, was a footway or walk, called an *allure* or *rampart-walk*, from which arrows and other missiles could be shot at an enemy below. At one corner of the roof was a watch-tower, from which a good view of the surrounding country was obtained, and on which a beacon fire could be lighted in times of danger.

Houses that had no moats, or only dry ones, were often protected with towers at the four corners, together with a *barbican*, or strong tower, placed to guard the main doorway.

Wells of water were considered of such importance, especially in case of siege, that they were frequently placed in separate towers, called *well-towers*, the entrances to which were locked and carefully guarded.

Many fortified manor houses, with moats, embattled walls, and gatehouses, were built long after the need for them had ceased to exist. Even in the sixteenth

Embattled Walls

century, with peace and prosperity all over the land, it was the fashion to build country houses with defences that were no longer needed.

At the Record Office in London can be seen a large number of the licences that were granted to certain lords of the manors, giving them permission to embattle the walls of their houses.

What we may call " domestic " manor houses, or those that were not fortified, were for many years very simple buildings, composed of a large hall with a few private rooms at one end and the retainers' quarters at the other end. The first change from this simple oblong building would be to add more rooms at each end, and after a certain length had been reached a turn was made, and so a courtyard was gradually evolved with the various buildings grouped around it.

As this courtyard kept much of the sunlight from reaching the rooms the custom arose of building rooms above those on the ground floor. Such rooms were at first called *solars*, meaning " sun-rooms," and they were mainly used as bedrooms, which were reached by outside stairways. Sometimes a chapel was added.

We have very few manor houses that remain as when first erected, and they may all be said to have grown rather than to have been built. For example, the small manor house of a Norman lord would be enlarged in the reign of Edward I, and perhaps almost entirely re-built when Henry VII was King, and again added to in the days of Elizabeth. It was in the reign of this queen, with the coming of peace and prosperity, that many moats were drained and laid out as gardens, that windows were enlarged, and that gatehouses were

ABOUT MANOR HOUSES 9

A Moat

pulled down, leaving these old houses much as we see them to-day.

The materials used for buildings of all kinds in the

THE PARTS OF A MANOR HOUSE

Middle Ages were always those that were cheapest and near at hand; no money was spent in bringing materials from a distance. Where stone was plentiful it was used, and where little stone was to be had, as in the Eastern Counties, many fine houses were built of brick.

In the chalk districts the walls were frequently faced with flints, cut and trimmed, and a number of good buildings treated in this way may be seen in the chalk districts of Kent and Sussex. But even when other materials were abundant, wood was always so convenient, especially when a house was wanted in a hurry, that it was continually employed, and in country districts to-day old timber houses are perhaps more common than those of any other kind.

The first drawing in this chapter shows two views of the fine old manor house still standing at Ightham Mote, in Kent, and the illustration *A Moat* is taken from one side of the same house. The entrance to a fortified house (p. 34) is from the Moat House at Appleby, in Leicestershire, and the embattled walls are those at Alnwick, in Northumberland. The last illustration gives a good idea of the appearance of a manor house from the courtyard after passing through the great gateway. This is from Little Wolford Hall, in Warwickshire. All these houses are in the style called *Tudor-Gothic*, excepting the half-timbered parts, which were added in the reign of Elizabeth. The windows in these later parts, it will be noticed, are much larger than those in the earlier portions.

During the last few years a large number of the smaller manor houses have been made into farmhouses, and with the breaking up of large estates into small

A Manor House

holdings the manor houses have ceased to fulfil the same social functions as formerly.

Several of the larger houses also are being adapted

THE PARTS OF A MANOR HOUSE

for purposes other than those for which they were built, as Canford Manor (Dorset), one of several manor houses that have been turned into public schools. Canford was the seat of Lord Wimborne, who converted an old manor house, dating from the reign of King John, into a modern mansion, now one of the most beautiful schools in the country.

The historical interest of our old English manor houses, begun some of them in the reign of the second Edward and finished in the days of the Tudors, is so great that we may regard them as among the most valuable links in our island story. They have come down to us from the days when mail-clad warriors awakened echoes in the stone-flagged courts, and sturdy cavaliers ducked their heads as they cursed at the narrow doorways.

It is good to visit an old manor house like Ightham Mote in Kent. We never tire of rambling through panelled halls and paved courtyards, or of wandering at will in the sweet old gardens, the flowers gay and bright, the hedges neat and trimmed, the grey old pile beside them dark and still, and soon we get to love and reverence these ancient homes of our native land, which breathe the spirit of an age with which we have entirely broken; while as for the nameless builders of these massive walls and sturdy towers, may we never cease to venerate their memory.

> "Their swords are ruste, their bodys duste,
> Their souls are with the Saints, we truste."

CHAPTER II

The Hall

FROM Saxon days until the end of the fifteenth century the hall was the most important part of a manor house. It was the chief room of the house, and around it all the other rooms were grouped.

In the great hall the lord of the manor held his courts, and there his retainers and serfs sat at the one long table for their evening meal. After the fifteenth century, with the springing up of large and prosperous cities and the founding of trade gilds, many village craftsmen flocked to the cities, and the nobles no longer kept up the same state of grandeur in their castles and manor houses.

The farm labourers, too, had become more independent, and as they gradually became possessed of homes of their own, there was not the same need for them to seek their meals at their lord's table as they had previously done.

It is not easy for us to-day to picture to ourselves one of these great halls, with a large household sitting down for a common meal, the retainers and servants in the body of the hall, the master and his guests on the raised platform, or dais, at the end. With the passing away of this common meal, this jovial gathering

14 THE PARTS OF A MANOR HOUSE

Bay Window of Hall

THE HALL

of serf and noble, both the spirit and the meaning of the old hall were lost beyond recovery.

Many halls were partly screened off, and behind the screens the serving of meals and carving was done, while at the back of the screens were doorways leading to the pantry, the buttery, and the kitchen. Above the screens was a music gallery or loft for minstrels, always an important feature of an old hall. This gallery generally had a separate entrance from the outside, so that the musicians could reach it without having to go through the hall.

In addition to a large raised hearth for burning logs, fireplaces were often built in the walls. Sometimes these were enriched with panelling and at other times painted with coats of arms. The open timber roofs of many halls are very fine and quite as good as those to be found in the churches of the same period. The roof of Trinity College, Cambridge, is an excellent example, and that at Christ Church Hall, Oxford, is almost equally good, as is also that at Westminster School.

The hall-flooring was usually of paved tiles which, being in many colours, were laid in patterns; but the earliest floors, like those of old cottages and farmhouses, were laid with large *flagstones* and covered with rushes. Beneath the floor of the hall were various vaults and cellars.

We must remember that these old halls did not look so bare in those days as they do to-day. The walls, whether of stone or panelled with wood, were hung with rich tapestries to a height of eight or ten feet. These hangings were often brought from abroad and cost large sums of money. The pegs on which the

16 THE PARTS OF A MANOR HOUSE

A Hall

THE HALL

tapestries were hung can still be seen on many walls, although the tapestry has disappeared.

All around the hall were stags' antlers for hanging coats and hats upon, while on the boarding at the end, and perhaps over the fireplace, would be swords and lances, hunting-horns and dog-whips.

The bay window was at first quite small, but it became larger and more imposing as the country became more peaceful. A few halls had two such windows, one at each end, but the usual position for a bay window was at the back of the dais. The beautiful bay window shown is at Fawsley Park. It is placed in the middle of one side of the hall, which is rather an uncommon position. This is a very fine window, with the flat surfaces or faces of the arch, called *soffits*, richly panelled, as also is the ceiling.

When the lord of the manor no longer took his evening meal with his household, many old halls were

THE PARTS OF A MANOR HOUSE

divided into two parts by a screen. One of these parts was used as a dining-hall and the other part as a *withdrawing-room*, or as we now say, drawing-room. Chiefly, however, the hall became smaller owing to the growing importance of other rooms, and with the building of " solars " and bedrooms, the hall was no longer used as a sleeping apartment, as had been the custom from Saxon days. The large hall never entirely disappeared, even in Elizabeth's days, but with an ever-increasing demand for privacy and comfort it became of less importance than formerly.

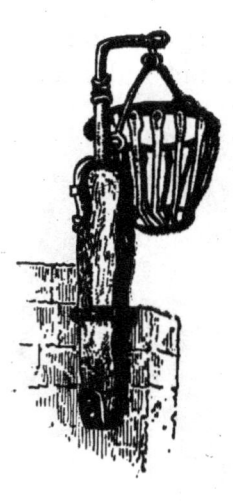

CHAPTER III

The Kitchen and Offices

AS one would suppose, when a large household was fed in the hall of a manor house, the kitchen was generally a big building, placed at a short distance from the hall.

Near the kitchen, and opening out from it, would be the *larder*, the *buttery*, and the *pantry* ; while beneath it was the *cellar*. In those early days there were no shops in the country and very few in the towns, so that large quantities of food had to be stored up in the houses, and even the richest lord of a manor had little to rely on in the way of food beyond the produce of his own estate.

When the kitchen was placed under other rooms it was generally vaulted, or built on arches, and some fine kitchens of this kind can be seen at Warwick Castle, and at the Prior's House, Wenlock, in Shropshire. Old manor-house kitchens usually have very large fireplaces, which sometimes have projecting hoods over them. Such fireplaces needed to be large when oxen and sheep were roasted whole, and not cut up into small joints before cooking as they are to-day.

Near the kitchen, and usually at the lower end of the hall, were the pantry and buttery. In the pantry

THE PARTS OF A MANOR HOUSE

A Kitchen

the bread was given out, and in the buttery the liquors were served. Within easy reach of the kitchen also were other small chambers like the lardarium, the salsarium, the bakehouse, and the brewhouse. In the lardarium was kept the potted meat for winter use, the mouths of the pots being covered over with lard.

The salsarium was the room in which the salted food and fish were kept as a reserve supply in case of siege or other emergency. The bakehouse was often near the kitchen, and it had its own ovens for the baking of bread and other foods. The brewhouse was always an important part of an old house. In it was brewed the malt liquor for the use of the household.

The kitchen illustrated is a very fine one at Stanton Harcourt. It is built in the form of a tower with a timber roof, and the original fireplaces and oven remain. This is one of the finest old kitchens we have left. The fireplace is at Chale, in the Isle of Wight.

Among the other important parts of a manor house

THE KITCHEN AND OFFICES

would be the *dairy*, the *granary*, the *mill*, and the *stables*.

The dairy was, of course, used for the same purposes as it is to-day—the storage of milk and eggs and the making of butter. The granary was the large barn in which the corn was kept after it had been threshed in a smaller barn. In the granary also would be stored the malt and hops for brewing.

A mill was essential at a time when the corn grown on the estate was eaten on the spot, and when bad roads made it difficult to send it any distance to be ground. The same stream of water that filled the moat would turn the mill-wheel.

In the days when all travelling and transport were performed by horses, stables were of the greatest importance, and they usually formed a part of the house itself, so that the horses could not be taken away or otherwise interfered with in times of danger. When the stables did not form a part of the house itself, they were placed either in the inner court, as at South Wraxall, or in the outer court, as at Tisbury.

It may be remarked here that nearly every part of a modern house can be traced back to olden times. Thus, our dining-room is but a smaller hall; the " withdrawing-room " is a larger solar; the " lord's chamber " exists in the library or study; and the " lady's chamber " in the dressing-room, or *boudoir*.

The buttery and pantry are now rolled into one and given the name " pantry " in houses and " buttery " in colleges. The cellars exist as they did formerly, and we cannot say that the kitchen is of less importance to-day than it was in past ages.

With the growth of brewing and baking into great

22 THE PARTS OF A MANOR HOUSE

trades, the private brewhouse and bakehouse have vanished, and as the butcher calls at our house every day for orders, we have no need to lay up stores of provisions in a lardarium or a salsarium. Lastly, we shall find that stables for horses remain in country districts, but in towns they have mostly been turned into garages.

STEPS IN COURTYARD

CHAPTER IV

Gatehouses and Chapels

EVERY old manor house had a gatehouse, through which those going to and from the house had to pass. Sometimes, as we have seen, this gatehouse was strongly fortified, and at other times it was a picturesque little building, without defences, giving entrance to the courtyard.

All our cathedrals and monasteries once had gatehouses, of which many remain, as do those at the colleges of Oxford and Cambridge. In the gatehouse lived the Warden, or officer whose business it was to question all those wishing to pass through.

We have a survival of the old gateways in the lodges of country houses. Where a large mansion has several drives leading to it a *lodge*, or small cottage, is placed at the entrance to each of them. In one of these lodges the gardener lives, in another the gamekeeper, and in yet another the coachman or chauffeur. The lodge-keepers, or their wives and children, open the gates for visitors, and close them securely at night, just as the wardens and porters opened and closed the gates of the old manor houses.

In fortified houses it would be the duty of the officer in charge to raise or lower the drawbridge and work

24 THE PARTS OF A MANOR HOUSE

A Gatehouse

GATEHOUSES AND CHAPELS 25

the portcullis or iron grating. The gateway illustrated is from a charming little manor house at Pokeswell, in Dorset. It is built of brick, and the room above the entrance arch is reached by a flight of stone steps placed inside the wall. The style of this little gatehouse is called *Jacobean*, from its having been built, like the manor house it guards, in the reign of James I.

The brick wall surrounding this house is a singularly beautiful one, and it shows that the old masons gave a considerable amount

A Chapel

of care and time to the building of such a commonplace thing as a wall.

In olden days no manor house was complete without its private chapel, or *oratory*, which was generally reached by a short passage leading from the hall. The

26   THE PARTS OF A MANOR HOUSE

lords of the manors, in addition to attending the services in the parish churches, always had morning and evening prayers read in these chapels, and at these

Bay Window

prayers the retainers and servants, as well as any guests staying in the house, were expected to be present.

Some of these private chapels are very beautiful

GATEHOUSES AND CHAPELS

little buildings, as the one illustrated. This is at Ightham Mote, in Kent, and, like the house to which it belongs, was built in the reign of Henry VII. It remains to-day exactly as when first erected, with its cradle roof, screen, and choir stalls, all of oak, and is one of the best private chapels we have left dating from the early part of the sixteenth century.

Wall Window with Dripstone

Oriel Window

CHAPTER V
Doorways and Windows

A GOOD strong doorway was essential to an isolated manor house, for on the security of the door the safety of the household depended. The doors of the fortified houses were very strong, and in addition to bolts and locks they were often protected with a portcullis or iron grating, although this is a defence found more often in castles proper than in manor houses.

In what we may call " domestic " manor houses, that is, those that were not fortified, the doorways were still very strong, especially those of the gatehouses that gave entrance to the courtyards beyond. The doors themselves were usually made of oak, banded with iron and fitted with enormous locks and bolts. The doors of gatehouses were generally fitted with a small hatch, or with a sliding panel, through which the porter could see who was knocking without opening the door.

Some of the best doorways we have left date from the time of Elizabeth, as the one illustrated. Here we see a little entrance porch of half-timbered work, with a flooring of tiles, and benches on each side. This pretty doorway is at Shakespeare Hall at Rowington, in Warwickshire, and tradition says that in a little room

30   THE PARTS OF A MANOR HOUSE

A Doorway

DOORWAYS AND WINDOWS 31

above it William Shakespeare wrote some of his plays, hence the name given to the house.

It has already been explained in the first book of this series, that windows were at first nothing more than small openings made in the walls to admit air rather than to give light, and what applies to cottage windows is equally true of those of manor houses. As time went on, and the country became more peaceful, windows gradually got larger, but for many years they were very small, both in churches and houses; and as a rule we shall find that the smaller the windows the older the house.

Glass was at first very dear, but when it became cheaper and less of a luxury, it was used to fill the apertures that had hitherto been protected with oiled linen, horn, and wooden shutters. In many old household accounts the cost of such alterations is given, as when Lord Howard, at Colchester, had to send to London for his glazier, who received 4s. 8d. for fourteen days' labour.

The greatest care was taken of glass windows, as we learn from the Household Book of the Duke of Northumberland, wherein we read that when that nobleman was not living in his town house in London, the glass windows were taken out of their frames and carefully laid by.

The windows were divided by mullions and transoms into several lights, each of which had its separate casement, or frame. These casements appear to have been made to fit different windows, not only in the same house, but in different houses also, so that when a family removed from one manor house to another the glass casements formed part of the movable goods.

32 THE PARTS OF A MANOR HOUSE

Entrance Tower

DOORWAYS AND WINDOWS 33

In the reign of Henry VIII, when glass had become much cheaper, all window casements were deemed to be part of the fixtures of a house, as they are to-day. We are told by several old writers that, except in churches and noblemen's houses, glass windows were rare before the time of Henry VIII.

During the reign of Elizabeth glass became comparatively cheap, with the result that the windows of many houses and churches were made as large as possible, as at Hardwick Hall, in Derbyshire, of which people said:

"Hardwick Hall,
More glass than wall."

Similarly, the windows of the Church of St. Thomas at Salisbury are so large that the building has the appearance of being composed of vast sheets of glass, held in place by slender strips of stone framework.

The principal windows in manor houses were *bay* windows, *wall* windows, and *oriel* windows. The bay window, as we saw in Chapter II, was generally large, and used only in the hall or other important apartment. It always projects, or stands out from, the face of the wall, as you will see by the illustration, which is the outside view of a window at Lytes Carey, Somerset. Another drawing is of a wall window divided into four lights by two strips of stone called *mullions* and one cross strip called a *transom*.

Above this window is a "hood-mould," or dripstone, the purpose of which is to protect the window from rain running down the face of the wall. All church windows of any size have these dripstones, which always follow the shapes of the window-heads.

34   THE PARTS OF A MANOR HOUSE

The oriel window is a small window that formed a recess for and gave light to the altar of a chapel or oratory, and its usual position was in the second storey, and not on the ground floor.

Entrance to Fortified Manor House

CHAPTER VI
Chimneys and Fireplaces

IT is perhaps as well to repeat here what was said in *The Parts of a Cottage*, that in early days the fire was made on an open hearth on the floor of the hall or other room and the smoke escaped either through the door or by an outlet in the roof.

Although chimneys were first built in this country by the Normans, they would only be used in the houses of the wealthy, and many years passed before they became common. Thus, William Harrison, writing in the year 1577, tells us that in his own village in Essex there were not more than two or three chimneys.

There is no doubt that in the fifteenth century the chimneys of many town houses were made of wood. In one of the Ordinances of the City of London, compiled in 1419, it is declared " that no chimney shall henceforth be made unless it be of stone, tiles, or plaster, and not of wood, under pain of being pulled down." The more wealthy of the citizens of London began to use coal in the reign of the first Edward, when the Mayor and citizens were allowed to levy a toll of sixpence upon every shipload of coal passing under London Bridge. As coal gradually took the place of wood for fuel in the larger country houses, chimneys became more

36 THE PARTS OF A MANOR HOUSE

numerous, although the open firehearth continued to be used for the burning of logs of wood and peat.

When the open fireplace was made in the middle of the floor of a hall, it was generally raised on a low platform of brick or stone and fitted with *andirons*, across which logs of wood could be placed, as you will see by the illustration of the old hall fireplace still remaining at the manor house of Penshurst, in Kent.

FIREPLACE AND OVENS

These old andirons can still be found in many old farmhouses, where large logs of wood are still used for fuel

For many years chimneys were only used in castles and large houses, and it was not until the end of the fourteenth century that wall fireplaces began to take the place of the open hearth on the floor. At first chimneys were single, but as time went on and brick came more into use, they were frequently *clustered*, or placed in groups, with very pleasing results.

The earliest chimneys were built of stone, but during the reigns of Henry VII and Henry VIII they were

Carved Mantelpiece

38   THE PARTS OF A MANOR HOUSE

mostly made of brick and richly moulded, a fashion that continued throughout the reign of Elizabeth. On no part of an old manor house did the masons spend more care than on the chimneys.

When the large fireplaces in the walls were bricked in at the sides to make them more suitable for the burning of coal, they were often fitted with elaborate *firebacks*, like the one shown. Large numbers of these beautiful firebacks still remain in Sussex, and they date from the days when this southern county had a great reputation for the excellence of its iron-work—that is, from the middle of the sixteenth century.

With the increase of chimneys and the building of fireplaces in the walls, chimney-pieces, or, as we now say, mantelpieces, came into use. Like the windows these were not at first regarded as fixtures. They were merely hung over the fireplace in such a way that they could be taken down when the owner of the house was absent.

When these mantelpieces were made of stone they became most ornamental, especially those in the hall or banqueting-room; and in the reign of Elizabeth, when mantelpieces of carved wood came into fashion, they were often very magnificent pieces of carpentry.

The illustration given is of a fine wooden mantelpiece at the manor house of Birt's Morton, in Worcestershire. As you will see, it extends from the floor to the ceiling, and is richly carved with the arms of various owners of the house. The grate is modern, but the other part is just as it was when made. On each side of this fine chimney-piece you will notice the thick silken ropes that were used for ringing the bells in the servants' quarters.

CHIMNEYS AND FIREPLACES 39

Above this fireplace will be seen a small portion of the plaster ceiling of the room. This will give some idea of the beautiful ceilings that were placed in manor houses during the reigns of Elizabeth and James I.

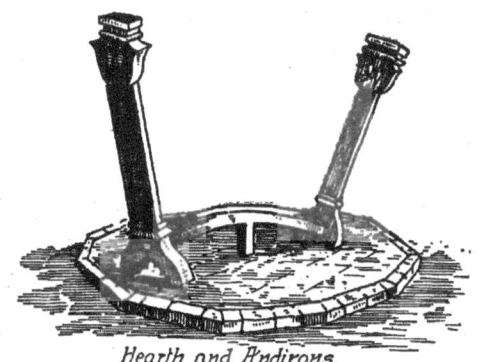

Hearth and Andirons

Fireback

CHAPTER VII
Stairways

THERE is not a great deal to tell about stairways, except that in early days, when solars and bedrooms began to be placed above the rooms on the ground floor, these upper chambers were frequently reached by stairways built outside the wall. External stairways were at one time very common in both small manor houses and cottages, and they generally had a little roof over them. The first inside stairways were in the form of strong ladders, and such were used for many years in castles as well as in houses.

In Norman days the *newel* stairway was introduced, and in many castles this was carried from the floor right to the top of the building, so that all the various rooms could be reached by it. As a rule, but not always, this kind of stairway was built of stone, the steps being placed around a central pillar, or newel, as you will see by the illustration of one of these stairways at Clenstone Manor House, Dorset. This shows exactly how the steps were placed in position. The great advantage of this kind of stairway was the small amount of space it occupied. Another very good example of a newel stair is that in the Tower of London, one of the few large fortresses built in the lifetime of the Conqueror.

STAIRWAYS

Outside Stairway

Newel Stairway

Straight-flight Stairway

42 THE PARTS OF A MANOR HOUSE

A Staircase

Many old church towers have similar stairways that lead to the belfries within them. Although what we call *straight-flight* stairways of stone were placed outside houses in Norman times, it was not until the days of Elizabeth that they were brought inside. The illustration is of a very interesting example, the earliest we have, at Beccles, in Suffolk. The steps here consist of massive blocks of oak, the ends of which are let into the solid wall. As rooms became larger stairways became more numerous, and when the steps were boarded up at the sides, the result was a real stair-case, a flight of steps enclosed at one or both sides

STAIRWAYS 43

in a case. It was during the reigns of Elizabeth and James I, that some of the most magnificent staircases were made, as the one illustrated at Aston Hall.

CHAPTER VIII
Dovecots and Sundials

AMONG the many picturesque features of an old manor house, nothing is more pleasing than the old stone or brick dovecot, around which large flocks of pigeons are always flying.

We cannot be sure when people in England first began to keep pigeons in dovecots, but it is generally agreed that William the Conqueror was the first to introduce into this country the large pigeon house, which, until the time of Elizabeth, only the lords of the manors and rectors were allowed to build. We cannot suppose that such a practical people as the Normans went to the trouble of building these great dovecots for ornamental purposes, or for any pleasure which the sight of large flocks of pigeons may have given them. It was the need for providing a reserve supply of food in case of emergency that led to the building of dovecots, wherein at least five hundred couples of pigeons could live and breed.

The earliest dovecots are of round formation, but the later ones are often square, six-sided, and sometimes octagonal, or eight-sided. But whatever

DOVECOTS AND SUNDIALS 45

the shape, all of them have the walls lined from floor to roof with nest holes, made in the thickness of the wall.

The first illustration is of a circular stone dovecot at the Court House, Richard's Castle. It is built after the Norman pattern, and has an imposing roof with three dormer windows. The walls are four feet thick and contain six hundred and thirty nest holes. Like

Dovecots

nearly all the round examples it is fitted inside with a large revolving ladder, so as to enable the owner to reach all the nest holes.

The other drawing shows an octagonal, or eight-sided, pigeon house, built in this case of brick, and dating from the seventeenth century. Here again the nest holes are made in the substance of the wall, which is two feet two inches in thickness. There is no

46   THE PARTS OF A MANOR HOUSE

revolving ladder, as such would be of no use in any but a round building.

Many of these old dovecots are fitted with a trap placed inside the top of the roof. This was worked by means of a hanging cord, and enabled any one using it to catch the birds as they entered.

Before the invention of clocks in the fourteenth century, sundials were placed on all kinds of buildings, as well as in the gardens of country houses. Sundials are of very great antiquity, and in the Book of Isaiah we read, " Behold, I will bring again the shadow of the degrees, which is gone down in the sundial of Ahaz, ten degrees backwards." This dial is thought to have come from Assyria about the year 714 B.C.

In China sundials are as common as clocks are in this country, and until a few years ago the Japanese used to carry small dials as we carry watches.

We know that the Romans placed sundials on temples, baths, houses, and on tombs but the oldest dial we have in England is that on Bewcastle Cross,

A Sundial

DOVECOTS AND SUNDIALS

which dates back to A.D. 670. In Norman times dials were placed at the junction of important highways for the benefit of travellers. For example, Seven Dials, in London, was so called because a column once stood there to which seven dials were fixed facing the seven roads that converged at that spot. It was not until the sixteenth century that sundials became fashionable in private gardens and over the doors of houses and churches. The pedestals of many sundials are of beautiful design and workmanship, as the two illustrated. These are both in Sussex, one being at Winchelsea and the other at Battle Abbey.

All old sundials bear mottoes, which are generally, as they should be, short and to the point, as the three following examples:

" Come, light ! visit me !
  I count time; dost thou ? "

" Light and shadow by turns, but always love."

" Haste ! oh, haste ! thou sluggard, haste !
  The present is already past.
  Begone about your business."

A Sundial

THE PARTS OF A MANOR HOUSE

In no place does a sundial look so well as in some old-world garden, where—

> " Serene he stands among the flowers,
> And only marks life's sunny hours ;
> For him dark days do not exist—
> The brazen-faced old optimist."
>
> GEORGE ALLISON.

THE PARTS OF A CASTLE

WRITTEN AND ILLUSTRATED
BY
SIDNEY H. HEATH
ART MASTER, PLYMOUTH COLLEGE
AUTHOR OF "PILGRIM LIFE IN THE MIDDLE AGES,"
"OUR HOMELAND CHURCHES," ETC., ETC.

LONDON

1929

CONTENTS

CHAPTER		PAGE
I.	About Castles	3
II.	Early Norman Castles	11
III.	The Keep	15
IV.	Edwardian and Later Castles	21
V.	The Barbican and other Defences	27
VI.	The Armoury	35
VII.	Chapels	39
VIII.	The Story of Corfe Castle	41

THE PARTS OF A CASTLE

CHAPTER I
About Castles

IT is not possible, in a small book of this kind, to make more than a passing reference to the early pre-historic strongholds, like Maidun Castle (Dorset), which were made, with an immense expenditure of time and labour, by piling up ramparts of earth divided by deep ditches or *fosses*.

These great camps were constructed for the defence of a large community, and they may be regarded as serving the dual purpose of cattle stations in times of danger, and primitive towns where the inhabitants could do their work in security.

The steep slope of the banks, and the cleverly contrived entrances, rendered them impregnable in the days before siege operations were understood. They could only be captured by hand-to-hand fighting. These earthworks are mainly the work of the New Stone men and the Bronze Age men, although enlarged and strengthened by later races, who, even when they spread over the valleys, kept their hill-fortresses in good repair in order that they could fly to them when danger threatened. A strong stockade, or a hedge of thorns, crowned the innermost bank, or was placed around the edge of the plateau.

4   THE PARTS OF A CASTLE

These vast earthworks were of little use to the Romans, whose system of warfare, and knowledge of military architecture, were far in advance of anything known to the British.

In addition to the walls of dressed and cemented stone, with which the Romans surrounded their permanent camps and stations; they erected strong fortresses along the eastern and southern coasts (as at Colchester and Porchester), to guard against the attacks of the Saxon tribes.

They had also to build the two famous walls in the north to keep back the Picts and Scots. One of these walls was built by the Emperor Hadrian, and the other by the Roman General Agricola. A large part of Hadrian's wall, which extended from the Tyne to Solway Firth, is still standing. A fine Roman *amphitheatre*, or open-air place of amusement, called "Maumbury Rings," remains at Dorchester. It is oval in shape and occupies a space of 218 feet in length and 163 feet in width.

Probably the greatest difference between the prehistoric and the Roman forts was that while the former were isolated strongholds, the settlers in which were always raiding each others territory, the Roman stations were military posts connected by strategic roads, and so forming part of the organised system that was the keynote of Roman policy and the secret of Roman success.

Although the Saxons, who appear to have hated the idea of living within walls, threw up earthen ramparts around a few of their towns, their principal defences consisted of dykes, marsh-land, forests, and rivers, within which boundaries the various tribes

ABOUT CASTLES

Pre-historic Earthwork (Maidun Castle)

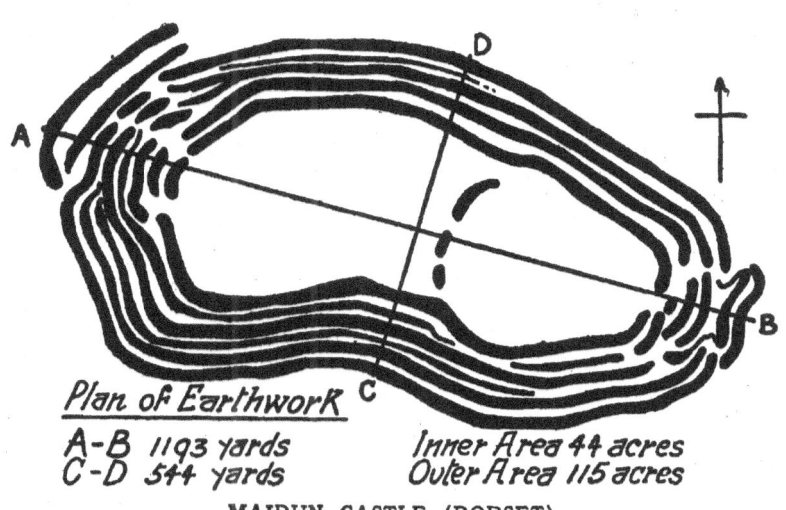

Plan of Earthwork
A-B 1193 yards   Inner Area 44 acres
C-D 544 yards   Outer Area 115 acres

MAIDUN CASTLE (DORSET).

THE PARTS OF A CASTLE

lived; and such strongholds as they may have possessed would, like the pre-historic camps, be communal in character.

The same may be said of the defences thrown up by the Danes, who, in the second period of their invasions, brought their wives and families with them; and it has now been firmly established that the "castle" proper for the defence of the individual, was practically unknown in England until it was imported from Normandy a few years before the Conquest.

In addition to castles erected by landowners to secure their territory and provide a safe dwelling-place for themselves and their families, many fortresses, as those at Old Sarum, Marlborough, and Ludgershall, were royal castles belonging to the Crown or held by constables, and supported by taxation. The bishops were great castle builders, and they, like the kings and the barons, often built castles to protect the townsfolk from whom they drew much of their income. However much the nobles may have despised the traders, they found them too useful to leave without protection, and the same applied to scattered villages, the inhabitants of which made contributions of *castle-guard* rent to the castle of their district.

At Castleton, Derbyshire, in 1158, a porter and two watchmen were paid £4 10s. jointly by the Crown. In 1160 at Rockingham Castle a porter and two watchmen received a yearly salary of £4 11s. 4d.; and at Worcester, in 1163, the only watchman employed was paid £1 10s. 5d. a year.

These salaries appear to have been paid by the Crown to the sheriffs of the counties in which the

MONMOUTH CASTLE (RESTORED).

castles were situated. In some castles watchmen and porters seem to have been the only officials in permanent residence. The watchmen lived in the upper room of the keep, so that they could give signals of approaching danger by blowing a horn, ringing a bell, or lighting a beacon fire ; so that those who had been taxed for the building, repair, and maintenance of their local castle, could find shelter within it until the danger was past.

Ignoring the pre-historic fortresses, and the camps of the Romans, Saxons, and Danes, we shall find that the castles of England fall into six well-defined groups. (1) The Motte and Bailey Castle. (2) The Rectangular Keep. (3) The Shell Keep. (4) The Transition-Norman Castle. (5) The Edwardian Castle. (6) The Castle-residence, in which the domestic element is about equally balanced by the military. After this last the castles became more and more large palatial residencies in which the fortifications took a secondary place, or were used to keep up what may be termed " castle tradition."

The student may care to have the following classification of defensive works drawn up by the Committee of *Ancient Earthworks and Fortified Enclosures.*

    A. Fortresses partly inaccessible, by reason of precipices, cliffs, or water, additionally defended by artificial works, usually known as *promontary fortresses.*

    B. Fortresses on hill-tops, with artificial defences, following the natural line of the hill, and known as *contour fortresses.*

    C. Rectangular or other simple enclosures, in-

PORTCULLIS AND DRAWBRIDGE

THE PARTS OF A CASTLE

cluding forts and towns of the Romano-British period.

D. Forts consisting only of a mound with encircling moat or fosse.
E. Fortified mounds, either artificial or partly natural, with traces of an attached court or bailey.
F. Homestead moats, such as abound in some lowland districts, consisting of simple enclosures formed into artificial islands by watermoats.
G. Enclosures, mostly rectangular, partaking of the form of F., but protected by stronger defensive works, ramparted and fossed, and in some instances provided with outworks.
H. Ancient village sites protected by walls, ramparts or fosses.

The headpieces of the chapters show some of the old castles as they appeared before they fell into ruins, or were destroyed.

CHAPTER II

Early Norman Castles

THE Normans, who landed on our shores in 1066, were, like the Romans before them, few in number as compared with the native population; and it being at all times, but especially then, a difficult matter to recruit the forces of an invading army, it was essential to adopt every available means to economise the expenditure of military force.

The Normans overcame this difficulty by the erection of small strongholds, or " motte and bailey " castles, all over the land. The average height of the mounds is forty feet, and the average area of the baileys, three acres. The first of these castles were erected at Richard's Castle and Ewyas Harold, by Norman barons to whom Edward the Confessor had given estates in Herefordshire.

When the mound had been thrown up a small " donjon," or keep of wood, was built on its flattened top, and at its foot a moat was made where a supply of water was available. The bailey also was surrounded by a moat or by a dry ditch and wooden palisades. The citadel formed the home of the lord, while huts and sheds in the bailey housed the retainers and stores.

THE PARTS OF A CASTLE

A MOTTE AND BAILEY CASTLE

A ladder of wood went from the outer edge of the mound-moat to the citadel. These small forts protected the household from enemies, while the citadel on the mound gave the lord security from his discontented retainers. The first change would be to substitute a stone wall for the outer palisading, which was liable to destruction by fire. In a few cases the wooden citadel also was replaced by one of stone, as at Christchurch and Plympton, but in the majority of cases wood, being cheap and easily procured, was retained for the inner buildings.

Remains of these mound and bailey castles can still be seen all over the country—Ongar, Stafford, Plympton, Okehampton, Wallingford, Stafford being but a few of the seventy-two thrown up during the eleventh century; and they constituted, as Mrs. Armitage* tells us, "the first links in the long chain with which the Normans established their hold on the land."

* *The Early Norman Fortress in England.*

EARLY NORMAN CASTLES

TRANSITION-NORMAN KEEP
(RESTORED) CONISBOROUGH

These little castles were followed by massive rectangular keeps which remained until the close of the twelfth century, when they gave way to those of round formation, known as "shell" keeps, as we shall see in another chapter.

We have also a few examples of keeps like those at Conisborough* and Orford (illustrated), which represent the transition from Norman to Early English. This type of castle was much favoured in France, but it was rarely used in England, the two illustrated being our best

* The illustration of this keep is based on that given in *Mediæval Military Architecture*, by G. T. Clark (1884), and the illustration of Harlech Castle (p. 22) is drawn from the same source.

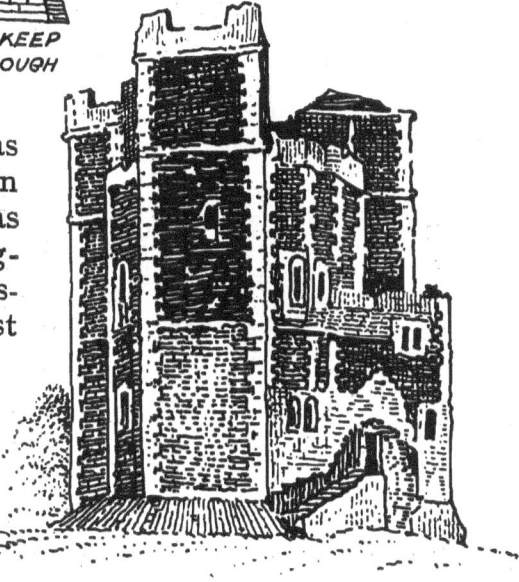

RUINS OF TRANSITION-NORMAN KEEP, ORFORD

THE PARTS OF A CASTLE

examples of these cylindrical keeps, which were also built at Brunless and Tretower.

TATTERSHALL

CHAPTER III

The Keep

ALTHOUGH some writers differentiate between what they call "domestic" keeps and "military" keeps, we must remember that all keeps (with the exception of those castles inhabited only by watchmen) were domestic keeps, since they formed the residence of the castle owner and his family; and this is true of a small "motte and bailey" fortress as of a massive building like the "King's Tower" at Corfe.

The keep, which is often termed the "castle," was but a part of a series of fortifications, a portion only of a vast stronghold; and resorted to by the garrison in times of pressing danger.

A castle was made up of a central building, or keep; upper and lower wards, or baileys, with walls, gates, barbicans and ditches, intended to promote the general safety.

Some castles occupied a considerable area. Norwich covered a space of twenty-three acres, and Lincoln almost as many, as no fewer than one hundred and sixty-six houses were pulled down to clear the ground for its erection.

The site chosen was usually an elevated spot

often protected by nature on two or more sides, and, excepting where the ground was very precipitous, a ditch, or a moat, was made around the enclosure. On the inside of the ditch a strong wall or curtain was raised. This was sometimes thirty feet high with a thickness of from six to eight feet. Occasionally there were two, or even three walls, each provided with a moat, as was the case at Norwich. Immediately within the outer walls were the garrison buildings and store - rooms. The keep itself was often placed in the centre of the fortification, as at Norwich, London, and Newcastle; but at Porchester it is on an angle of the castle wall, and at Richmond it secures the entrance into the outer bailey. The keep was usually placed upon ground higher than the rest of the fortress, and sometimes a faced mound was made from the material taken out of the ditches. The general form of the earlier Norman keeps nearly approached a square, and in castles of the larger class, a small tower is attached to the main structure to defend the entrance.

A RECTANGULAR KEEP
ROCHESTER.

THE KEEP

ENTRANCE TO KEEP, ARUNDEL.

The cautious policy of the Normans suggested that the doorway of the keep should be at a considerable elevation, but exceptions occur at Colchester and Bamborough, where the doorways are on the ground floor.

As a rule the doorway was in the second storey; at Newcastle it is in the third, and in large castles the doorways were often protected by small towers at the sides.

Where windows are introduced they are merely loop-holes in the lower storeys, but they become larger in the upper ones. At Newcastle the windows of the third storey are provided with double lights, which could be closed with shutters in times of siege.

In large keeps the interiors are usually divided into two or three compartments by strong stone walls, rising from the ground to the top of the building. The white tower in the Tower of London is divided into three sections, and the interior of Rochester keep into two. The floors of each storey, excepting the

THE PARTS OF A CASTLE

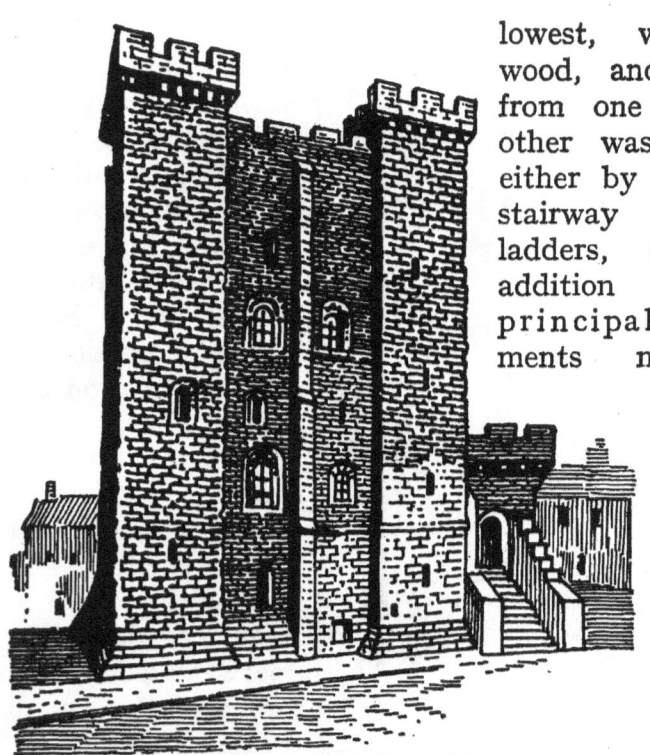

THE KEEP OF NEWCASTLE

lowest, were of wood, and access from one to the other was gained either by a newel stairway or by ladders, and in addition to the principal apartments numerous small chambers (or garde-robes) were made in the thickness of the wall.

Fireplaces are found in some keeps but not in others. Rochester has one in each of the larger rooms. On the other hand, none have been found in the keep of Richmond, and only one in the Tower. It is possible that charcoal braziers were used where no fireplaces existed.

Wells of water were essential if a castle were to maintain a siege, and the needs of the garrison required that water should be obtainable in the topmost storeys.

THE KEEP

THE RUINED KEEP OF CORFE

At Rochester the pipe from the well goes from the ground to the top of the building, and a similar arrangement existed in the keep of Carlisle Castle.

The storey in the keep which was called the hall was the general living- and sleeping-room of all the inmates, excepting perhaps the heads of the household, who may have sought a certain amount of privacy on another floor of the building.

Such was the general character of the Norman rectangular keeps, which lasted until the close of the twelfth century, when the round or "shell" keeps began to be built, after a few experiments had been tried, as at Orford, where Henry II built the polygonal keep already alluded to.

THE PARTS OF A CASTLE

A SHELL KEEP

With the improvement of engines of war like the battering ram, the corners of towers and keeps became vulnerable, and the salient angles were also liable to destruction by sap and mine.

The round keep (having no corners) was easier to defend and it would also deflect heavy missiles.

Both types of castles remained until we come to the keepless fortresses of the Edwardian era, which are regarded as the masterpieces of mediæval fortifications.

Remains of rectangular keeps exist all over the country, as at Rochester, Norwich, Newcastle, Richmond, Ludlow, Corfe, to mention but a few. Shell keeps were probably more numerous at one time than those of square formation, but they have been much altered, and are rarely found in anything like their original state. They were built, among other places, at Ongar, Berkeley, Carisbrooke, Totnes, Restormel, and Windsor.

CHAPTER IV

Edwardian and Later Castles

THE term "Edwardian" has been applied to that style of concentric fortress which followed the keep-castle, and carried forward the art of fortification to the Decorated period of English architecture; and although the fortress of Caerphilly was planned on concentric lines before Edward I came to the throne, it is to him we owe the magnificent castles of Conway, Caernarvon, Harlech, and Beaumaris.

In these buildings the keep, the principal feature of the earlier castles, was dispensed with, and in its place came a gatehouse-castle placed in a square or an oblong court, encircled by a strong wall with towers at the angles. Every part of these castles was suitable for daily use, and no portion was set aside as a last resort for a hard-pressed garrison. They may be termed gatehouse-palaces, in which the hall was the principal living-room, although the domestic element was still subordinated to military needs.

Caernarvon (1), and Harlech (2), are illustrated. Harlech is shown as it appeared when first built; but Caernarvon is in much the same condition to-day as it was when completed.

22 THE PARTS OF A CASTLE

AN EDWARDIAN CASTLE (1)

CAERNARVON.

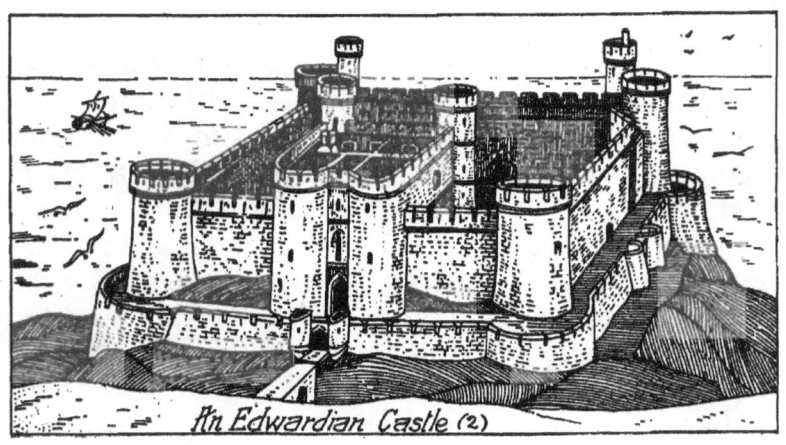

An Edwardian Castle (2)

HARLECH (RESTORED).

EDWARDIAN AND LATER CASTLES 23

We are now nearing the time when domestic comfort was beginning to encroach more and more on purely military requirements, and of this type of castle Kenilworth is about as good as any we had; and one that stands mid-way between the Edwardian

Ruins of Conway Castle

THE PARTS OF A CASTLE

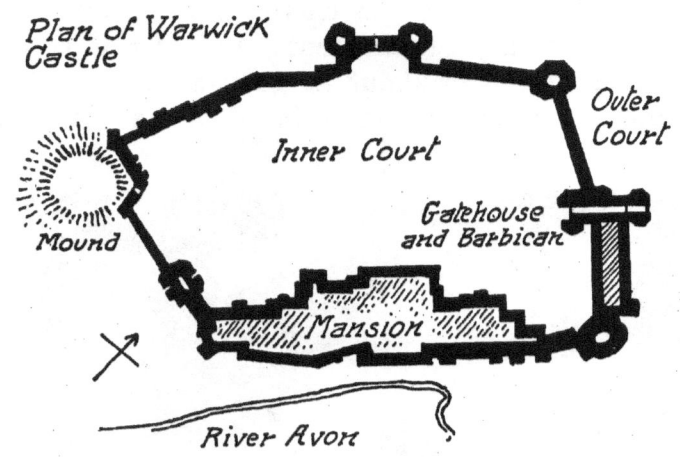

TOWER AND BARBICAN
WARWICK

EDWARDIAN AND LATER CASTLES 25

fortress, and the castle-mansions of Warwick and Hurstmonceaux, in which domestic comfort and military needs are about equally balanced. When first built, each of these castles combined a palatial residence with an impregnable fortress.

The vast castle of Warwick was erected partly at the end of the fourteenth century, but not completed until the fifteenth, and even to-day the walls, barbican, towers, and battlements remain perfect. Looking at the plan, we see the dwelling-house protected by the river on one side, and by the fortifications on the other sides. This stronghold was originally a "motte and bailey" castle, of which the mound remains outside the northern tower.

Berkeley Castle is another good example of the same period, and almost as perfect, although differing in plan.

We have a few rather eccentric buildings which might almost be called "toy" castles, as the one illustrated of Tattershall Castle,* Lincs., and built about the middle of the fifteenth century.

Here we have a Norman keep treated in a Gothic manner, with corner turrets, and battlements; the whole surrounded by a moat. The large size of the windows, however, indicates that this castle was not built for serious defence.

Warkworth Castle, and Middleton Tower, Norfolk, are other examples of these moated towers, which have much in common with the pele-towers of Ireland and Scotland, in that they were fortified dwellings.

Tattershall Castle was built by Ralph Cromwell, lord High Treasurer of Henry VI. The bricks of which

* See p. 14.

26 THE PARTS OF A CASTLE

RUINS OF KENILWORTH CASTLE

it was made came from the fens of Holland to the sister fenland of Lincolnshire. In 1911 the castle was sold to an American, and in September of that year it was taken down brick by brick prior to its removal to the United States, thus proving at once the efficacy of wealth, and the poor patriotism with which we guard our precious heritage.*

We thus see that the castle proper began with the " motte and bailey " type, and ended with the castle-mansion of Warwick, after which came a large number of beautiful residences, with defensive attributes tacked on more for embellishment than for practical purposes.

* During the process Tattershall Castle was bought for the nation by the late Lord Curzon, and such portions of the edifice as had been removed were replaced and the whole structure carefully restored.

CHAPTER V

The Barbican and other Defences

THE Barbican was usually an outwork for the better defence of a gate or drawbridge, and it may be likened to a narrow lane walled in at the sides, as may be seen by the illustration of the exterior of the barbican at Walmgate-bar, York, and the interior of that at Warwick Castle. Others are at Carlisle, Alnwick, and Richmond castles.

Grose, an old writer, says " To begin from without, the first member of an ancient castle was the barbican. It had no positive place, except that it was always an outwork, and frequently advanced beyond the ditch ; to which it was then joined by a drawbridge, and formed the entrance into the castle. Barbicans are mentioned in Framlingham and Canterbury castles. For the repairing of this work, a tax called *barbecanage* was levied on certain lands."

Bodiam Castle has a small defence called the barbican, and Carlisle Castle had one covering the main gate. At Bridgnorth the barbican contained a kitchen. There is a street in London, near Redcross Street, called the Barbican from a watch-tower that stood there. Milton once lived in the Barbican,

THE PARTS OF A CASTLE

BARBICAN OF TOWN GATE, YORK.

INTERIOR OF BARBICAN
WARWICK.

and Spelman, the antiquary, died there in 1640. Plymouth also has a street called the Barbican.

Spenser, in the *Faerie Queene*, has:

" Within the barbican a porter sate,
Day and night duly keeping watch and ward."²

In the time of Henry V, an unknown writer, describing the fortifications of Harfleur, says :—" Before the entrance of each of the three gates, the

THE BARBICAN AND OTHER DEFENCES 29

prudence of the enemy had erected a strong defence, which we term a barbican," and Lydgate says in his *Story of Thebes* :—

" And made also by werkmen that were trew,
Barbicans and bulwerkes, strong and new,
Barreres, chains, and ditches wonder deepe,
Making his anow (vow) the city for to keepe."

The *Sally-port* was an important part of a castle. Whilst the attention of the besieging forces was concentrated upon a particular point, like the storming of the main entrance, a detachment of the beleaguered garrison would issue out by some concealed doorway, and attack them from the rear. It was of course essential that, whilst the sally-port was so planned as readily to admit the returning garrison, it should as readily exclude the foe. Sally-ports were generally very narrow, with a number of sharp turns, and so dark inside that they could be traversed only by those familiar with their peculiar construction.

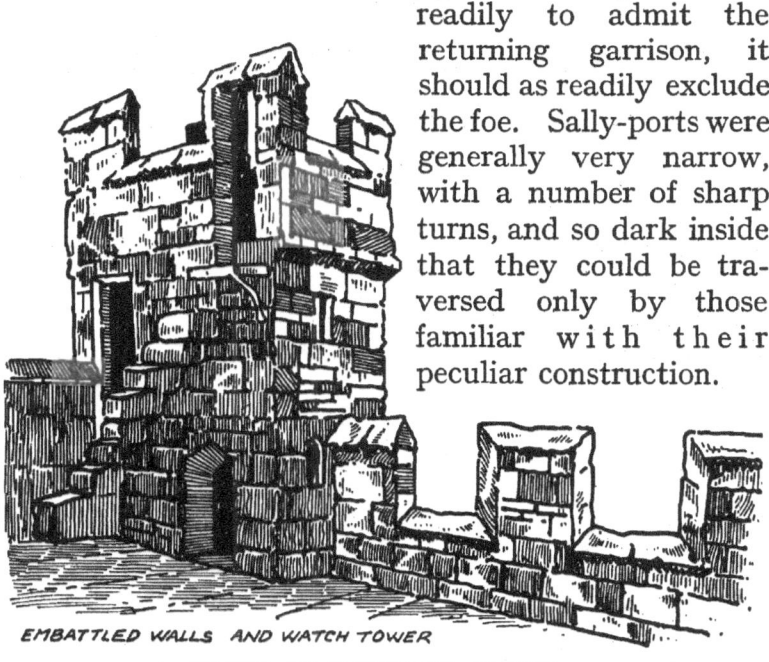

EMBATTLED WALLS AND WATCH TOWER
BASED ON NAWORTH CASTLE.

30 THE PARTS OF A CASTLE

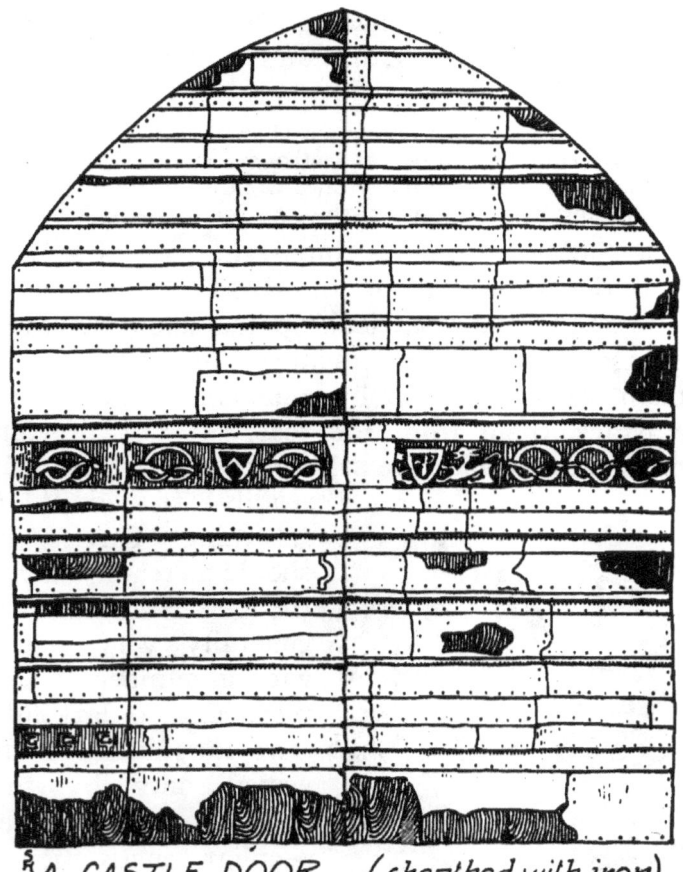

A CASTLE DOOR (sheathed with iron)
MAXTOKE.

The *Battlement* is a parapet on the top of a wall, having notches in it from which arrows and other missiles could be discharged at besiegers below. The raised portions are called *merlons*, and the notches *embrasures*. Sometimes the merlon is pierced with a small opening called a *crenelle*. The merlon was for

THE BARBICAN AND OTHER DEFENCES 31

the purpose of protecting the soldier while discharging his weapon through the embrasure.

The *Alure*, or rampart-walk, is strictly the alley, passage or flat gutter behind a battlemented parapet, and wide enough to enable any one to walk round the tops of the walls.

The *Bartizans* were small projecting turrets, often of wood, and pierced with holes for archers to shoot through. Compton Castle, Devon, has a number of good examples.

The *Bailey* was the open space between the outer and inner lines of a castle or fort. When there were more than one they were known as the Inner and Outer Baileys. The name has survived in the " Old Bailey," London ; and in the Upper and Nether Baileys at Colchester.

The *Portcullis* was usually a strong-framed grating of oak, having the lower points shod with iron shoes. In the smaller gateways the whole was often of iron. The Portcullis was hung so as to slide up and down in grooves, and it was worked by heavy weights. Portcullises do not appear to have become general in England until the twelfth century, although they were used in Italy, for defence against the Saracens, long before that date. The Portcullis, or *altera securitas*, appears on the badge of the House of Somerset.

Castle doors were naturally as strong as they could be made. At Maxtoke Castle, Warwickshire, there are two of the original doors (one of which is illustrated), sheathed with iron. Each is five feet wide and twelve feet high to the point of the arch. Across the middle of the door runs a band of embossed

THE PARTS OF A CASTLE

A CASTLE STAIRWAY (WARDOUR)

DOORWAY IN THE TOWER

heraldic devices. These doors were made in 1346, the year in which the castle was built. In 1432, Lord Maxtoke exchanged his castle with Humphrey, Earl of Stafford (afterwards Duke of Buckingham), for Wishton and Wodeford, Northants. This is recorded by Dugdale, who also tells us:—" The Earl of Stafford caused the gates to be covered with plates of iron, and his arms, with those of his lady, to be embossed thereon, with two antelopes his supporters; and in further memory that the gates were strengthened and beautified by him, he caused the burning nave and knot, the ancient badges

THE BARBICAN AND OTHER DEFENCES 33

ROOM IN THE BEAUCHAMP TOWER, LONDON

of his ancestors, to be embossed in the ironwork."

We have abundant evidence that the working of iron and steel was much practised in this country long before the coming of the Normans. In the courts of the Saxon and the Welsh kings the chief smith was an officer of considerable importance, and one who enjoyed many privileges. In the Welsh court the king's smith had a seat next the chaplain, and he was entitled to a drink of every kind of liquor that was brought into the hall.

The drawbridge was an important, although minor, feature in castle defence, and the modes of working it varied. Usually, in small castles, chains were attached and passed through holes in the portals, the bridge being raised and lowered by weights or counterpoises. In large castles the arrangements were more complicated, and the working was done in a room above the gateway.

34 THE PARTS OF A CASTLE

Heading Block and Axe in the Tower

Where castles were situated on rivers, or had wide moats that could not be spanned by bridges, entrance was gained through "water-towers" by boats, as you will see by the illustration,* which is based on a drawing by Mr. W. D. Caroe, showing the Castle of Monmouth restored. The illustration of a "Portcullis and Drawbridge" † is explanatory, and is of no particular castle.

It is now generally agreed that the dungeons found in many old castles were Edwardian additions. The Normans had little use for these underground prisons. If they caught a foe worthy of serious attention they usually put him to death.

The castle stairway illustrated is at the old Castle of Wardour, Wilts., and it is known as the "Grand stair." This castle was built by Lord Lovel in 1392, by special licence from Richard II, and the entrance to the stairway is a Renaissance addition.

* See p. 7.   † See p. 9.

CHAPTER VI
The Armoury

BEFORE the invention of gunpowder the methods of attacking fortresses and walled towns were by catapults, slings, borers, and battering-rams; the soldiers working the last two being often protected by a pent-house, or small roof of wood or thatch.

Where there was no moat the ditch had to be filled in with earth or with hurdles before the gate could be reached, and when it was so filled, the uplifted drawbridge formed an additional barrier. A closed gate was attacked with battle-axe and fire; and whilst these modes of forcing an entrance were being applied, the garrison, from the battlements, were heaving heavy stones, and pouring hot lime, molten lead, and boiling oil, on to the casqued heads of their assailants.

The application of gunpowder for projectiles is thought to have originated in Italy about 1326, and the first mention of fire-arms in France occurs in 1338, on the breaking out of war between that country and England. The English are credited with having first used cannon for field pieces, as distinct from their previous use as siege guns.

From an Italian historian, Villani, we learn that the English army at Crecy had three cannon loaded with iron balls. The balls for large cannon were frequently of stone, or stone coated with lead, and large quantities of stone cannon balls came from the quarries of Kent.

The first cannon were very small, so small that the cannonier held the gun in his hand while firing it. The illustration (from a MS. of the reign of Edward IV) depicts a soldier holding one of these cannon as he applies a match to the touch-hole. After a few discharges the metal would become too hot to hold, so later the gun was attached to a wooden stock, and in this way originated our modern rifles and guns.

When the match was applied to the touch-hole by a trigger, this addition (an Italian invention) gave rise to the "match-lock." The "wheel-lock" was another Italian invention.

The earliest large cannon were hooped, and the first cannon to be cast in one piece was made by Ralph Hogge, at Buxted, Sussex, in 1543. News of this achievement soon reached the Continent, and large orders came from the French, who returned the compliment with interest when they bombarded Sussex coast towns with guns of Sussex make.

This resulted in the government taking bonds of £1,000 from the owners of the Sussex furnaces in order that no cannon should be exported without licence.

In a castle armoury were kept armour, bills, cross-bows, daggers, battle-axes, pikes, and other military weapons. The armoury in the Tower is a very fine one, as also is that at Warwick Castle.

The sword, as a fighting weapon, has a place and

THE ARMOURY 37

HAND CANNON

WITHOUT STOCK   WITH STOCK

dignity of its own, far above that of any other lethal weapon. With the sword alone many men have carved their way to fortune or to fame. Some ancient swords are engraved on the blades with mottoes, such as, " Do not draw me without reason : do not sheath me without honour."

It is with the sword, the aristocrat of fighting weapons, that the King to-day confers the honour of knighthood on his subjects.

From the time of the Crusades to the sixteenth century, armour was worn only by the mounted knights ; and the retainers, who were foot soldiers, were badly armed and poorly equipped until the trained bands of archers were organised.

The arms and armour seen to-day in castle armouries and museums were used until the invention of fire-arms rendered

38 THE PARTS OF A CASTLE

them obsolete, or caused them to be retained for purely ornamental purposes, as with the helmets and breastplates of our Lifeguards.

CHAPEL IN THE TOWER
LONDON

Gateway of Neath Castle

CHAPTER VII
Chapels

A CHAPEL seems to have formed an integral part of a feudal castle, and it ill accords with our modern ideas of consistency to find buildings so replete with contrivances for the slaughter and the torture of the foe, so well provided with chapels for the performance of religious duties.

An unknown writer has said of the Normans :—
" To pray for mercy one hour, and be most merciless the next ; to glorify the Giver of all good, as the most fitting preparation for the dispensation of all evil ; to enshrine their hopes of salvation on the altar of Christ, while they pressed forward to the mortal end of all through an almost continuous life of rapine, violence, and strife."

We often find two chapels, one in the bailey for the general household, and the other a private oratory in the keep, and reserved for the orisons of the lord and his family. At Newcastle the chapel is under the stairs, and is a building of singular beauty as

THE PARTS OF A CASTLE

compared with the rest of the fabric. At Colchester the chapel is a spacious apartment of great massiveness; while that in the White Tower (London) is the finest and earliest castle-chapel we have. It is large, and has a nave, aisles, and apse, all vaulted.

The chapel had no special position. At Castle Rising it is on the first floor of the keep; and at Guildford and Brougham it was in the wall. At Prudhoe it was over the gateway.

Occasionally it is a detached building standing in the principal court, as at Ludlow, where, however, only the circular chancel (illustrated) remains. Ludlow Castle was the early residence of Edward IV, and the cradle of his infant sons.

A CASTLE CHAPEL (CHANCEL ONLY)

LUDLOW

CHAPTER VIII
The Story of Corfe Castle

FEW things are more interesting than the history of an old feudal castle, even when it is now in ruins, for that very circumstance impresses upon the mind the varying fortunes with which it has been so long associated, and the leading events that have marked its career.

Situated in the very heart of Purbeck (Dorset) and surrounded by low, green hills, stands Corfe Castle, probably the strongest mediæval fortress (with the exception of the Tower of London) ever erected in this country. The site is one which is secluded as lying in a valley, but has all the advantages that an isolated hill affords.

That there was a fortification here in Saxon days is possible, although not a trace of pre-Conquest work remains. The castle, as shown by the illustration, was begun by the Normans, and finished by later builders, the imposing residential keep being built long after the walls and towers.

In 948, King Edred gave the hill on which the castle stands to the Abbots of Shaftesbury, who kept it until 1075, when it was given to William the Con-

THE PARTS OF A CASTLE

queror in exchange for the church of Gillingham. The outer wall of the castle was built as near the edge of the hill as possible, and every few yards massive round towers were built into it. The entrance consisted of a gateway tower flanked by side towers. The moat was dug around the foot of the hill and filled with water from a neighbouring stream.

As the plan given shows, the space *intra muros*, or within the walls, was divided into baileys or wards, each of which was a stronghold in itself.

The first ward was supplied with a well of water, and a bridge across another moat led to the Castle Ditch, said to have been cut by order of King John. Beyond the ditch is a steep rocky hill on the top of which stood the imposing buildings of the keep, rising far above the other portions of the castle. Just within the gateway leading to the second ward was a stone stairway that led directly to the King's Tower. This second ward was triangular in plan, and protected by three towers, two round, and the third, at the apex, octagonal ; which last was used as a prison for criminals and persons of low rank. A strongly-fortified gateway gave entrance to the third ward containing the keep. Here stood the King's Tower, eighty feet high, and with a wall twelve feet thick. At one time this tower was used as a State prison. Around the tower were grouped the numerous domestic buildings, and on the opposite side of the ward was the Queen's Tower, connected with the Banqueting Hall and with the kitchens. The fourth ward was of small dimensions, and at its eastern end was a garden with another well of water.

That the murder of Edward the Martyr (the details

THE STORY OF CORFE CASTLE 43

Corfe Castle in 1643

of which are too familiar to be repeated here) took place on or about the spot where Corfe Castle now stands is generally admitted. The Anglo-Saxon Chronicle tells us that the cruel deed took place at *Corfesgate*, where stood Elfrida's house, probably a small wooden building of which all traces have

THE PARTS OF A CASTLE

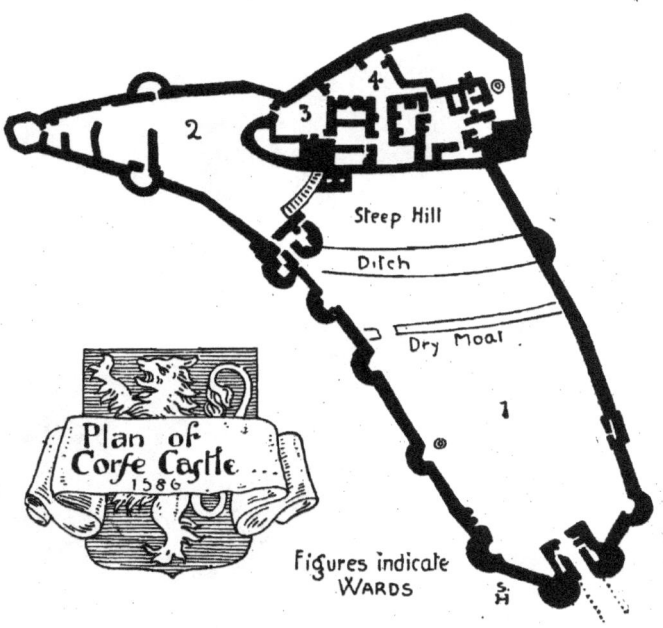

vanished; and although we may not know the exact spot where Edward received the fatal dagger-thrust, we do know that his body lay for one year at Wareham, in a chapel displaced later by the present parish church. In the English Chronicle, under date 979, we may read :—" In this year was King Edward slain at even-tide at Corfegate, on the 15th before the Kalends of April, and then was he buried at Wareham, without any kind of kingly honours."

And again under date 980 :—" In this year St. Dunstan and Alfere, the earldormen, fetched the holy king's body, St. Edward's, from Wareham, and bore it with much solemnity to Shaftesbury."

THE STORY OF CORFE CASTLE   45

When she heard of Edward's death, Elfrida retired to Bere Regis, near Dorchester, where she lived in seclusion. We have few records of Corfe until the reign of King John, who had several hunting-lodges in Dorset. When this monarch realised that the barons were getting restless under his misrule, he moved his court, his crown jewels and regalia, to this strong Dorset Castle, which, a little later, he turned into a State prison. After Prince Arthur of Brittany had been put to death at Rouen, his sister Eleanor, and twenty-two others of noble birth were taken to Corfe, and here Eleanor died after forty years of captivity. During her imprisonment she had as companions in misfortune, Margery and Isabel, daughters of William, king of Scotland. On the death of John, Corfe passed to the Earl of Pembroke, the guardian of the nine-year-old king, Henry III; and shortly after Edward II came to the throne, workmen were sent from London to fit up the castle for his residence; but when he went there it was as a prisoner, pending his removal to Berkeley Castle, where he was foully murdered. In the time of Edward III, Corfe was held by the Earl of Kent, and then passed to several nobles in turn, including the unfortunate Duke of Clarence, who is said to have been drowned in a butt of Malmsey wine. Queen Elizabeth sold the castle to Sir Christopher Hatton, who commanded the Dorset ships that helped to destroy the Spanish Armada. The last important event in the history of the castle took place while it was in the possession of Sir John and Lady Bankes during the Great Civil War. In 1643, while her husband was away, Lady Bankes and a few serving men, held the castle for

THE PARTS OF A CASTLE

CORFE TOWN AND CASTLE

six weeks against the pick of the Parliamentary troops, and it was only through the treachery of Colonel Pitman, a Royalist officer who had been sent to help her, that the fortress fell. So struck were the Roundheads with the bravery of Lady Bankes, that she and the survivors were allowed to depart with the full honours of war; but the House of Commons passed a resolution ordering so strong a Royalist castle to be destroyed. The towers were blown up with gunpowder, or so undermined that they fell of their own weight. The ruins were then plundered, many Dorset houses were built with its stones; while the lead was sold to a plumber at Poole.

Even to-day the ruins are magnificent, although but fragments of the historic edifice of which they formed a part. Corfe town, now called a village, is a sleepy little place that seems content to live on the memories of other days, for never again can the stormy scenes of warfare, or the clash of sword and spear, bring to it prosperity or renown. The plan given of the castle has been drawn from one made by Ralph Treswell in 1586, and preserved, with many

THE STORY OF CORFE CASTLE 47

other relics, at Kingston Lacey, the present seat of the Bankes family.

" The Earth goeth on the Earth, glistening like gold,
The Earth goeth to the Earth, sooner than it would,
The Earth builds on the Earth, castles and towers,
The Earth says to the Earth, ' all shall be ours.' "

Shield of the Black Prince
in Canterbury Cathedral

www.ingramcontent.com/pod-product-compliance
Lightning Source LLC
Chambersburg PA
CBHW052212240426
43670CB00036B/200